50 Fairy Things to Make & Do

Contents

Dancing fairies

Draw pointed feet to make her dance on tiptoes.

1. Use a black pen to draw the fairy's arms, head, eyes, mouth and body. Add looping shapes for her skirt, then draw her legs and wings.

2. Fill in the skirt with a pink pencil. Then, draw pink circles on her cheeks and add a nose. Fill in her body with a purple pencil.

3. Draw two ovals inside the end of each wing. Draw some lines from the ovals to her body, then fill the wings with light shading.

4. For the fairy's ballet shoes, fill in the tips of her toes with a black pen. Then, add some crosses going up her legs for ribbons.

Chalk fairy

1. Cut a triangular-shaped skirt from white tissue paper, then rip it along the bottom. Glue the skirt onto a piece of dark blue paper.

2. Use white chalk to draw the top layer of the skirt on top of the tissue paper. Then, draw white lines inside the shapes for pleats in the skirt.

3. Cut another piece of tissue paper for the body and glue it on. Then, draw the fairy's wings in chalk on either side of the body.

4. Rub the chalk to smudge the wings and make them look transparent. Then, draw around them again and add little lines inside, too.

5. Paint the fairy's neck and head, then paint two thin lines for arms. Paint lots of wavy yellow lines for the fairy's hair, like this.

6. Draw a white line for the wand and paint a yellow star at the end. When it is dry, draw her eyes, nose, lips and cheeks with felt-tip pens.

11

Glittery boxes

1. Mix some white glue with a little water. Then, cut bright tissue paper into small pieces.

2. Brush a box and lid with glue. Press tissue paper pieces onto the wet glue, overlapping them.

3. Brush on another layer of glue and add more tissue paper. Add more layers, then let the glue dry.

4. To make 'sequins', punch lots of holes in some shiny paper. Then, empty the hole puncher onto a plate.

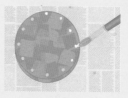

5. Using the tip of a paintbrush, dab blobs of glue around the edge of the lid. Press on the sequins.

6. Brush a spiral of glue on the lid, then sprinkle glitter over it. When it is dry, shake off any excess glitter.

7. For a 'gem', dip a piece of tissue paper into the glue. Roll it into a ball, then roll it in some glitter.

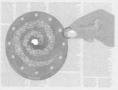

8. Let the gem dry. Then, dab a blob of glue in the middle of the spiral and press on the gem.

Try adding different glitter shapes, such as a star, onto the lid.

13

Fairy castle

Leave a space between the two towers.

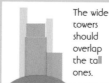

The wide towers should overlap the tall ones.

1. Cut a hill and two tall, thin towers from tissue paper. Glue them all onto a piece of thick paper.

2. Cut a bright pink tower and glue it on. Cut and glue on two short, wide towers, above and beside it.

3. Cut and glue on three blue and lilac towers. Then, cut lots of very thin tissue paper strips.

Leave a space for the flagpole.

4. Trim the strips to fit across the towers. Glue them on. Cut and glue on seven small rectangles, too.

5. Cut out pointed roofs and glue them on. Then, cut out flags and glue them above the roofs.

6. Cut a door and a round window and glue them on. Cut bushes and glue them onto the hill.

7. Draw windows with felt-tip pens. Use a gold pen to add details such as flagpoles and bricks.

8. Cut four paper strips, two as tall as the paper, and two as wide. Glue them on as a frame.

9. Glue tissue paper circles on the frame, for roses. Add leaves, then decorate them all with a gold pen.

Sugar Plum Fairy

Leave some space above the head.

1. Using a pencil, draw a head, neck and bodice on thick white paper. Draw an oval for the skirt.

2. Draw the fairy's arms, wings, wand, face and hair. Then, add legs, overlapping the skirt a little.

3. Brush watery pink paint all over the fairy. The pencil lines should show through. Let it dry.

Make tiny folds to gather the paper.

4. Using thick paints, fill in the fairy, but don't paint her skirt or the bottom part of her body.

5. Rip an oval of purple tissue paper for the skirt. Glue it on so that it overlaps the tops of the legs.

6. Cut a strip of pink tissue paper. Gather it along one edge, then glue this edge along her waist.

Shake off any excess glitter when the glue is dry.

7. Cut a bodice from pink paper. Cut a 'V' in the top, then glue it on so that it covers the top of the skirt.

8. Draw over her lips, nose, eyelashes and cheeks with pencils. Then, draw her ballet shoes with pens.

9. Brush glue on her wand and in a line across her waist. Sprinkle glitter over the wet glue.

Tulip card

1. To make a card, fold a piece of thick yellow paper in half, with its long edges together. Then, press firmly along the fold.

2. Draw some tulip shapes on bright paper and cut them out. Then, draw the same number of stalks on green paper and cut them out.

3. Glue the stalks at different heights onto the card. Make them overlap the bottom edge. Then, trim off the ends, like this.

4. Spread glue over the backs of the tulips. Then, press them onto the ends of the stalks, making some of them overlap each other.

Pretty star wand

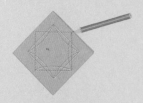

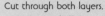
Cut through both layers.

1. Fold a piece of thin cardboard in half. Draw a square on it and add curves inside the edges.

2. Turn the cardboard a little. Then, draw another square over the first one. Add curves, as before.

3. Draw around the outline of the curves with a red pencil, to make a star. Then, cut out the star.

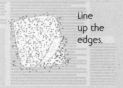
Line up the edges.

4. Fold the stars in half. Draw a curved triangle on the fold and cut it out. Then, unfold all the shapes.

5. Lay the middle pieces on book covering film. Draw a border around them. Cut out the shapes.

6. Peel the backing paper off the film. Sprinkle glitter over one, then press the other shape on top.

Decorate both sides.

7. Tape a long piece of gift ribbon to one end of a straw. Wrap it tightly around and around, then tape it.

8. Tape the straw onto the side of the star with pencil lines. Tape the sparkly shape over the hole.

9. Tie gift ribbon onto the straw, below the star. Glue the other star on top, then glue on sequins.

Fairy wings

1. Draw two big and two smaller wings on paper. Cut them out, then lay plastic foodwrap over them.

2. Rip up white tissue paper. Overlap lots of pieces on the plastic, covering the wings and their edges.

3. Mix white glue with water to make it runny. Then, brush it over the pieces of tissue paper.

4. Add a layer of ripped pieces of pink tissue paper and glue. Then, add two more white layers.

5. Sprinkle glitter on the wet glue. When it is dry, brush a layer of glue over the top. Let it dry.

6. Peel off the tissue paper. Lay the paper wings on top, draw around them and cut out the shapes.

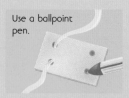

Use a ballpoint pen.

7. Glue the top parts of the wings onto the bottom parts. Decorate the wings with sequins.

8. Make four holes in a small cardboard rectangle. Thread two long ribbons through the holes.

9. Glue the rectangle onto the back of the wings, with the ribbons sticking out. Let the glue dry.

Fairyland painting

1. Lay some paper towels on an old newspaper. Then, spread red or pink paint on the paper towels with the back of an old spoon.

2. Cut a potato in half, then carefully cut away the two sides to make a handle, like this. Press the bottom of the potato into the paint.

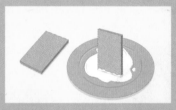

3. Press the potato onto a piece of paper. Then, dip a finger in white paint and print some spots. Using a brush, paint a white stalk.

4. To print daisies, cut a small piece of thick cardboard. Dip the end of the cardboard into white paint, then press it onto the paper.

5. Print more white lines crossing over each other. Paint a yellow dot in the middle, then add green stalks and leaves, too.

6. Finger paint some fairies. Print their arms and legs with a piece of cardboard. When the paint is dry, draw their faces with a black pen.

Holly fairy collage

Fold

Use paper from a magazine.

Join the points in the middle.

1. Rip a shape for the fairy's skirt from pink paper. Then, glue it onto a large piece of paper.

2. Fold four pieces of green paper, for wings. Draw half a holly leaf on each fold. Cut them out.

3. Unfold the leaves and flatten them. Then, glue them just above the top of the fairy's skirt.

4. Rip a white tissue paper shape that is a little bigger than the skirt. Gather it at the top, like this.

5. Glue the gathered part onto the skirt. Then, cut a body from white paper and glue it on top.

6. Cut out a head, neck and some hair and glue them together. Glue them on and draw a face.

7. Rip sleeves from paper, then cut out arms, feet and shoes. Then, glue on all the pieces.

8. Cut a crown from pink paper and a strip of white paper for a wand. Glue them onto the fairy.

9. Add a star sequin or sticker at the end of the wand. Then, decorate the dress with paper circles.

Hearts card

1. Spread white glue on a strip of paper. Then, sprinkle glitter over the wet glue and leave it to dry.

2. Cut a vase shape and a heart from two shades of bright paper. Glue the heart onto the vase.

3. Cut three small paper hearts and three bigger ones. Glue the small hearts onto the big ones.

Put your thumb here.

4. Cut the glittery paper into three strips. Then, glue the hearts onto the ends of the strips.

5. Cut three pieces of gift ribbon. Tape them to the back of the vase. Then, tape on the strips, too.

6. To curl a ribbon, hold it against closed scissors, then pull it across them, like this. Curl all the ribbons.

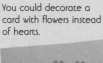

You could decorate a card with flowers instead of hearts.

7. Fold thick paper to make a card. Glue on the vase, then bend the glittery strips over.

8. Draw lots of hearts on shiny paper. Cut them out and glue them on. Glue on sequins, too.

Paper flowers

Don't tape it more than halfway up.

1. Draw half a heart on a folded piece of paper. Then, cut out the shape, through both the layers.

2. Unfold the shape and lay it on thick paper. Draw around it four times, then cut out the hearts.

3. Tape a straw near the bottom of one heart, like this. Squash the end of the straw as you tape it.

Make the slots the same length.

4. Glue another heart over the straw. Tape four thin strips of paper near the top of another heart.

5. Glue the last heart over the strips, then cut a slot into it. Cut a slot down into the heart with the straw.

6. Hold the heart with the slot at the bottom above the other heart. Slot the hearts together.

To make tulips, cut out different shapes in step 1.

This shape makes a straight tulip.

This shape makes a curved tulip.

7. Draw a leaf on a folded piece of thick paper. Cut out the shape, then glue it onto the straw.

8. To curl the strips, bend them with your fingers. Then, thread small bright beads onto the ends.

31

Fairy tiara

Lay the foil shiny side down.

Press down hard.

1. Cut a wide strip of kitchen foil, longer than a pipe cleaner. Then, lay the pipe cleaner on top.

2. Squeeze the foil around the pipe cleaner. Roll it into a thin band, then roll it on a flat surface.

3. Cut five thin strips of foil, half the length of the band. Squeeze them into sticks and roll them.

4. Cut three flowers with four petals. Dab white glue on the tips and sprinkle glitter on them.

5. Cut out three larger flowers. Dab glue in the middle of them and press on the glittery flowers.

6. Curl one end of each foil stick into a spiral. Glue one spiral onto the middle of each flower.

Gently bend the sticks to make them wiggly.

7. Lay the flowers in a row, glittery side down. Lay the band halfway up the stems, like this.

8. To attach the flowers, bend the bottom of the stems up. Then, twist them around the band.

9. Twist the other foil sticks onto the band. Glue on sequins, then bend the band into a curve.

Flying fairies

Paint the hair overlapping the head a little.

Make the wings overlap.

1. For a fairy flying sideways, start by painting her head, then add her hair and dress. Paint wings above the dress, and a dot for the wand.

2. When the paint is dry, draw around her face with a thin black pen. Draw a nose and ear, then add her dress, feet and two pointed wings.

Draw the stick on either side of her hand.

3. Draw one arm on the dress and the other below her face. Draw a stick and a star for the wand. Then, add wavy lines for her hair.

For a fairy looking down, paint her body and wings above her head. When you add her face, draw her nose and mouth at the bottom.

Glittery unicorns

1. Dip your finger in white paint and finger paint a body. Finger paint a head and a neck, too.

2. For legs, cut a strip of cardboard. Dip the long edge in the paint, then drag it across the paper.

3. For a bent leg, print two lines with a smaller piece of cardboard. Use a corner to print ears.

4. Squeeze glitter glue down the neck. Use a corner of the cardboard to drag lines for the mane.

5. Squeeze lines of glitter glue for the tail and drag them to make them wispy. Then, add a horn.

6. When the glitter glue has dried, use a black felt-tip pen to draw an eye, nostril and mouth.

One end needs to stay sticky.

7. For the wings, cut two pieces of sticky tape and dip them into some glitter, like this.

8. Press the sticky ends of the tape onto the back. Fold them up, and cut off the corners.

Fairy door sign

Poppy's Room

Keep this piece for later.

1. Using a pencil, draw around a small plate on a piece of paper. Then, cut out the circle.

2. Fold the circle in half, then in half again. Open it out, then cut out one quarter, like this.

3. Draw two wings touching the folds. Cut around the wings and along the folds, like this.

Decorate the arms.

4. Decorate the fairy. Push the wings together, to curve the body. Glue them onto thick paper.

5. Draw and cut out a face and hair, then glue them together. Draw arms on the spare quarter circle.

6. Cut out the arms, then cut out hands and glue them on. Glue the arms and head onto the body.

Make one end rounded.

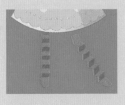

Poppy's Room

7. For legs, cut two long strips of paper. Then, fold each strip lots of times, to make zigzags.

8. Glue the zigzag legs under the body. Make sure the rounded ends are at the bottom.

9. Cut a heart shape around the fairy and write your name. Then, press on lots of shiny stickers.

Flower gift tags

1. Draw a square on a piece of white cardboard with a wax crayon. Then, draw a flower inside the square, with a spiral for its middle.

2. Fill in the flower and the background with different shades of runny paint, like this. The wax crayon lines will resist the paint.

3. When the paint is dry, cut around the square, leaving a painted edge. Then, tape a piece of ribbon to the back of the tag, like this.

On another gift tag, you could draw a flower with lots of petals, like this. Then, fill it in with different runny paints, as you did before.

Printed fairies

1. Glue a sponge cloth onto a piece of thin cardboard. This makes printing the fairies less messy.

2. Draw a triangle for the body on the cardboard. For the head, draw around a small bottle top.

3. Cut out the two shapes carefully. Then, lay some paper towels on top of an old newspaper.

Gently rub the cardboard each time.

4. Spread white paint on the paper towels. Press the sponge side of the triangle in the paint.

5. Press the sponge onto a piece of paper, then lift it off. Print a head, too, then print more fairies.

6. Cut two wings from thin paper for each fairy. Then, fold each wing in half and open it out.

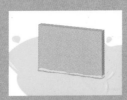

Leave room for the wings.

The wings stand out a little.

7. For the fairies' hair, press the edge of a piece of thick cardboard into some pale yellow paint.

8. Print their hair. Then, print their arms and legs with another piece of thick cardboard.

9. Paint hands and feet, and add faces. Spread glue on one half of each wing, and press them on.

Flower picture

The strips are for the sides of the frame.

1. Cut a rectangle of white tissue paper. Cut two cardboard strips a little longer than the paper, too.

2. Glue the strips onto the tissue paper. Cut strips for the top and bottom, then glue them on.

3. Fold a square of tissue paper into quarters. Draw two curves and cut along them. Open it out.

Rounded petals   Pointed petals

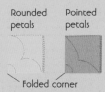

Folded corner

4. Fold two more squares of tissue paper into quarters. Draw shapes on each one, like this.

5. Cut along the lines, through all the layers. Open the flowers, then cut out lots more.

6. Glue the flowers onto the white tissue paper. Cut out and glue on tissue paper circles for middles.

7. Fold a strip of green tissue paper in half, twice. Cut a leaf shape through all the layers.

8. Glue on the leaves. Then, draw outlines around the leaves and flowers with a black pen.

9. Using the black pen, draw lines, circles and spirals on the flowers. Add lines on the leaves.

Fairy bug friends

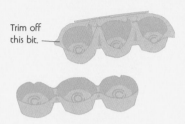

Trim off this bit.

1. Cut the lid off a cardboard egg carton. Then, use scissors to cut the bottom part of the carton into two pieces, along its length.

2. For the caterpillars' bodies, lay the pieces of egg carton on an old newspaper. Brush them with thick green paint, then let them dry.

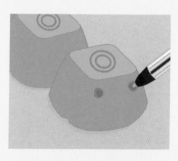

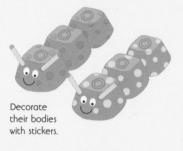

Decorate their bodies with stickers.

3. Using a ballpoint pen, carefully make two holes in the front of each caterpillar. Then, cut two short pieces from a drinking straw.

4. Push one piece of straw through each hole. Cut out white circles for eyes and glue them on. Then, draw the caterpillars' faces.

47

Frosted flowers

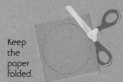

Keep the paper folded.

1. Fold a piece of tissue paper in half. Lay a mug on it and draw around it. Then, cut out the circle.

2. Lay the circles on a newspaper. Dab white glue around the edges, then sprinkle them with glitter.

3. When the glue is dry, push one end of a pipe cleaner through both circles, to make a stem.

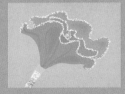

4. Slide the circles a little way down the stem. Pinch the tissue paper and twist it around the stem.

5. Secure the tissue paper to the stem with a piece of sticky tape. Open out the petals a little.

6. For a leaf, fold another piece of tissue paper in half. Draw a leaf shape, then cut it out.

7. Cut a pipe cleaner in half. Spread glue over one leaf. Then, press one end of the pipe cleaner onto it.

8. Press the other leaf on top. Spread glue over the leaf, then sprinkle the glue with glitter.

9. When the glue is dry, lay the leaf stem next to the flower stem, then twist them together.

Snowflake fairies

1. Draw around a mug on white paper, then on purple paper. Cut out the circles.

2. Fold the white circle in half, then fold it twice more. Cut a triangle from one side.

3. Cut out lots more triangles, all around the edges of the folded paper. Unfold the snowflake.

 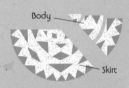 

Body

Skirt

Sash

4. Brush white glue over the snowflake. Sprinkle it with glitter and let it dry. Glue it to the purple circle.

5. Cut the snowflake in half. From one half, cut shapes for a skirt and a body, like this.

6. Glue the skirt onto a piece of paper, then glue on the body. Cut a purple sash and glue it on.

Fold

Keep the paper folded.

Add a crown and shoes, too.

7. For wings, cut out another circle and fold it as in step 2. Draw half a wing shape on the fold.

8. Cut out the wing shape. Cut triangles into the fold. Open out the wings, then spread glue on them.

9. Sprinkle glitter on the wings. Glue them on, then cut out and glue on a head, hair, legs and arms.

Hearts giftwrap

1. To make a stencil, fold a piece of thick paper in half. Draw half a heart against the fold, then cut along the line. Keep both pieces of paper.

2. Mix some red paint with white glue on an old plate. Then, spread the paint out on the plate a little with the back of a spoon.

Hold the stencil in place.

Don't move the stencil.

3. Lay the stencil on a large piece of thin paper. Dab a sponge into the paint. Then dab it over the heart, until the shape is filled with paint.

4. Before the paint has dried, sprinkle red glitter over the left half of the heart. Gently press the glitter on with your fingers.

5. Move the stencil and print lots more hearts, all over the paper. Sprinkle glitter on the hearts, then leave the paint to dry completely.

For a tag, lay the heart that you cut out in step 1 on some folded paper. Dab paint all over the tag, then sprinkle it with glitter.

Painted ice fairies

1. Cut a rectangle from a piece of thick cardbord. Dip one edge of it into some white paint.

2. Place the edge of the cardboard on some paper. Scrape it around to make a skirt shape, like this.

3. Dip the edge of a shorter piece of cardboard into the paint. Drag it across to make the body.

4. Mix paint for the skin. Dip the edge of another piece of cardboard into it, then print the arms.

5. Print a neck and two feet with a smaller piece of cardboard. Then, finger paint a head.

6. When the head is dry, dip a fingertip into blue paint and finger paint the fairy's hair.

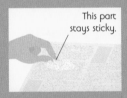

This part stays sticky.

7. For wings, hold a piece of sticky tape at one end. Dip it into glitter sprinkled on a newspaper.

8. Make a second wing. Then, cut a corner off each one, away from the sticky end, like this.

9. Press the sticky part of each wing onto the fairy. Fold back the wings and press them down.

Pretty heart bag

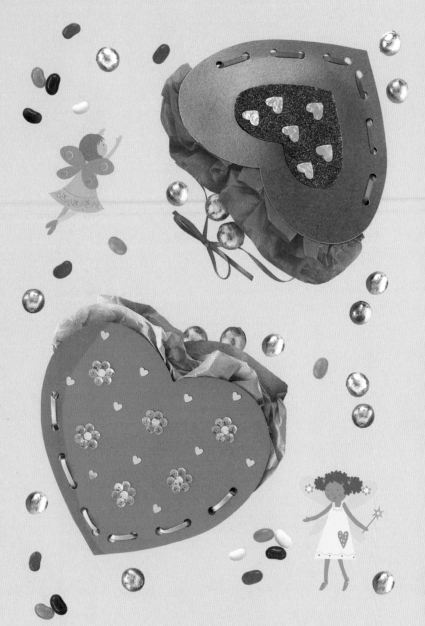

1. Fold a piece of paper in half. Draw half a large heart against the fold, then cut it out.

2. Unfold the heart, then lay it on thick paper. Draw around it twice. Then, cut out the hearts.

3. Fold the first heart in half again. Draw a second smaller half heart inside, then cut along the line.

Lay the hearts on a newspaper.

Dab on a blob of glue.

4. Unfold the small heart you have just cut out. Draw around it twice on paper. Cut out the hearts.

5. Brush white glue over the smaller hearts. Sprinkle glitter over them, and glue on sequins.

6. Glue the smaller hearts onto the big ones. Glue the points of the big hearts together, like this.

7. Using one side of a hole puncher, make holes up the sides of the heart. Don't make holes all the way up.

8. Cut a very long piece of thin ribbon, then thread it through all the holes, starting in the middle.

9. Fold two large tissue paper circles and push them into the bag. Then, tie the ribbon in a bow.

Painted flower

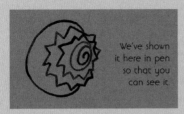

We've shown it here in pen so that you can see it.

1. Use a pencil to draw an oval for the middle of a flower. Add a small spiral on one side, with two zigzag circles around it, like this.

Wiggly line

2. Draw some petals around the middle. Then, draw a wiggly line inside some of the petals, to make it look as if they are curled over.

3. Draw a long stem with several leaves coming off it. Make the ends of some of the leaves look as if they are curling over, like this.

4. Mix some white paint with just a little water on an old plate. Then, using a thin paintbrush, carefully paint over the pencil lines.

Don't paint the ends that are curling over.

5. Starting at the middle of the flower, paint a thin white line out to the edge of a petal. Then, paint more lines to fill each petal.

6. Paint a white line down the middle of each leaf. Add lots of lines coming off it. Then, completely fill the stem with white paint.

Sparkly tiara

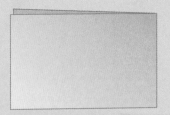

1. Cut a rectangle of thick paper that is long enough to fit around your head, with a little overlap. Then, fold it in half.

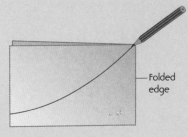

Folded edge

2. Using a pencil, draw a curved line across the paper. The pencil line should go to the top corner of the folded edge, like this.

3. Draw curly shapes like these below the pencil line. Add some against the fold, too. Then, carefully cut along the curly lines.

Only cut halfway into the paper.

4. Unfold the paper. Make a cut going down into it, a little way from one end. Then, make a second cut going up into the other end.

5. Decorate the tiara with sequins, beads and gold and silver pens. Then, slot the tiara together with its ends on the inside.

You could make a tiara like this one by drawing slanting lines in step 3.

Fairy paperchain

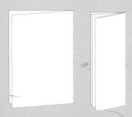

1. Fold a long rectangle of thin paper in half, with the shorter edges together. Then, fold it in half again. Crease the folds well.

2. Draw a fairy's arms and dress on the folded paper, making sure that the arms touch each side of the paper. Draw her hair, too.

Don't cut here.

3. Cut around the fairy, but don't cut the folds where her arms are. Then, carefully unfold the paper to make a chain of four fairies.

4. Fill in the fairies' hair and hands with felt-tip pens. Then, draw four faces on a separate piece of paper. Cut them out, then glue them on.

5. Draw stripes on the dresses with bright felt-tip pens. Then, cut strips of patterned paper from magazines and glue them on.

Cut out and glue on crowns, too.

6. Fold a piece of kitchen foil as you did in step 1. Draw wings against the fold, then cut them out and glue them onto the backs of the fairies.

Star card

Shake off the excess glitter when the glue is dry.

1. Draw three stars on a piece of yellow paper, making them all the same size. Then, cut out the stars.

2. Dab a blob of white glue onto the middle of each star. Then, sprinkle glitter over the wet glue.

3. Cut three strips of thin paper. Dab glue onto one end of each strip and press it onto the back of a star.

4. Fold a rectangle of thick paper in half, to make a card. Then, glue the strips onto the card, like this.

You could make a gift tag with one star on it.

5. Leave the glue to dry. Then, stand the card up, to make the strips bend and the stars fall forward.

Christmas fairy

1. Draw around a plate on pink paper. Cut out the circle, then fold it in half and open it out.

Fold

2. Draw a line from the middle of the circle to its edge. Draw a wing below it, touching the fold.

Cut here.

3. Cut along the fold, around the wing and along the line. Then, cut halfway down the wing, like this.

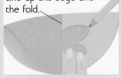

Line up this edge and the fold.

4. Bend the wing over and gently hold it down, like this. Draw around the edge of the wing.

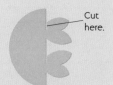

Cut here.

5. Open out the shape. Cut around the second wing, then cut halfway down into it.

6. Bend the body around and slot the cuts in the wings together. Curve the body with your hands.

7. Cut out a head, hair, arms and hands. Glue all the pieces onto the body, then draw a face.

8. Cut out legs and shoes and glue them together. Draw stripes on the legs. Tape the legs inside the body.

9. Cut a shiny paper crown and a wand. Glue them on, then decorate the fairy with sequins.

Sparkly frame

1. Lay the picture you want to frame on a piece of thick paper. Then, use a pencil to draw lightly around the picture, like this.

2. Draw another rectangle inside the first one. Then, push a sharp pencil through the middle of the smaller rectangle, to make a hole.

3. Push one scissor blade through the hole. Then, cut around the edge of the smaller rectangle to make a 'window' in the frame.

4. Cut strips of paper that are as wide as the frame. Then, cut the strips into squares and glue them around the frame, like this.

5. To make your frame sparkly, brush on spots of white glue and sprinkle them with glitter. Press on shiny stickers, too.

6. When the glue is dry, turn the frame over. Lay the picture face down and tape it in place. Then, tape on a loop of thread for hanging.

Flying fairy card

Make sure both cuts are the same length.

1. Cut a blue and a green rectangle from paper, making them the same size. Fold the green one in half.

2. Make two small cuts in the middle of the fold, to make a flap. Fold the flap to the front and back.

3. Open the card and push the flap through it. Close the card and smooth it flat, then open it again.

Don't glue the flap.

Shake off any excess glitter.

4. For the grass, draw a zigzag line across the card, above the flap. Then, cut along the line.

5. Fold the blue paper in half for the sky. Glue the green card onto it, with the middle folds lining up.

6. Cut out a pair of wings. Spread white glue on them, then sprinkle them with glitter. Let them dry.

Decorate her with glitter glue.

7. Cut a paper circle for the fairy's head. Cut a shape for her hair and glue it on. Then, draw her face.

8. Cut out a dress, arms and feet. Glue the arms, feet and head onto the dress. Then, add the wings.

9. Glue the fairy near the top of the flap. Then, cut out flowers and glue them on the grass.

Fairy collage

Use paint that isn't too runny.

1. For wings, lay a leaf on newspaper, with its veins facing up. Then, brush paint over the leaf.

2. Lay the leaf on tissue paper. Press firmly on it to print a leaf, then print six more. Let them dry.

3. Cut out the leaf prints. Then, cut a paper circle for a head and some hair from shiny paper.

4. Glue the hair onto the head, and draw a face. Then, cut a top and skirt from bright paper.

5. Glue the top onto the skirt. Glue three leaf prints onto the skirt. Then, cut a sash and glue it on.

6. Cut arms from paper. Glue them to the back of the body, then glue on four leaves for wings.

7. Glue the fairy onto a piece of paper, but don't glue down the bottom of her skirt. Glue on her head.

8. Cut out shoes from shiny paper and glue them under the skirt. Then, glue down the skirt.

9. Cut a crown and a wand from shiny paper and glue them on. Then, press on shiny stickers.

Paper lanterns

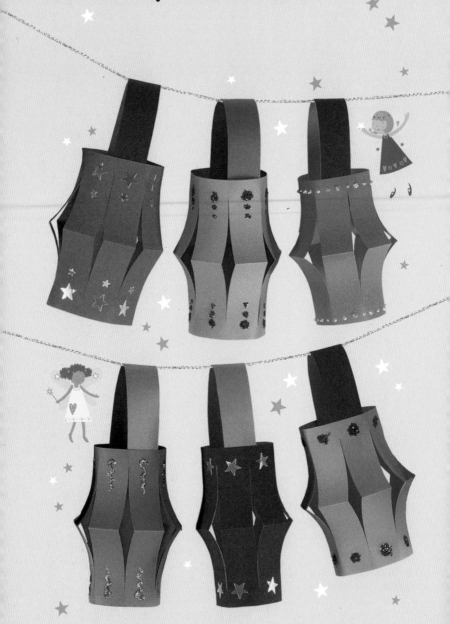

1. Fold a piece of thick paper in half. Then, cut along the fold to make two rectangles. Each rectangle can be used to make a lantern.

2. Fold one rectangle in half so that the long sides meet. Make cuts into the folded side, but don't cut all the way up to the top.

Spread the glue on this edge.

3. When you reach the end of the paper, cut all the way to the top, to make a narrow strip. This will be the handle for the lantern.

4. Open out the folded piece of paper. Spread glue along one of the short edges, then press it firmly onto the other short edge.

Glue the handle onto the inside.

5. Spread glue on both ends of the strip that you cut off in step 3. Press the ends firmly onto the top of the lantern. Let the glue dry.

6. Make another lantern from the other rectangle. Then, decorate both lanterns with stickers, glitter glue or paper shapes.

Ice castle collage

Glue the mountains along the bottom edge.

Make the road narrow at the top.

1. For mountains, cut pink paper triangles of different sizes. Make one bigger than the others.

2. Cut the tip off the big triangle. Glue the mountains onto a blue piece of paper. Add the big one last.

3. Draw a wiggly road on pale pink paper. Cut it out, then glue it onto the big mountain.

4. Cut out three tall towers and a wall. Glue them on, then cut out and glue on two short towers.

5. Cut a shiny paper door, windows and roofs. Glue them on. Add tiny windows with a silver pen.

6. Draw bricks. Then outline the bricks and windows with a silver pen. Glue on shiny sequins, too.

7. Pour some glitter and granulated sugar into a container, then shake it to mix everything together.

8. Dab white glue on the road, roofs and mountains. Pour the sugar mixture on. Shake off any excess.

9. Cut out a moon from kitchen foil and glue it on. Press silver star stickers onto the sky, too.

Flower pop-up card

1. For the card, cut two rectangles of paper the same size. Then, fold one of the rectangles in half, with its short edges together.

2. Make two small cuts into the middle of the folded edge, to make a flap. Fold the flap to the front, then to the back. Unfold the flap.

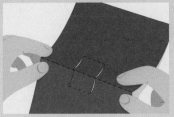

Don't glue the flap.

3. Open the card and push the flap through the fold, like this. Close the card carefully and smooth it flat, then open it again.

4. Fold the other piece of paper in half. Then, glue the two pieces of paper together, making sure that the middle folds line up.

The wax will resist the paint.

5. Cut a piece of paper the same size as the card. Draw a picture on it with wax crayons, then brush runny paints over the top.

6. Decorate the inside of the card, too. Then, when all the paint is dry, cut out the picture. Glue it onto the front of the flap.

Fairy Queen picture

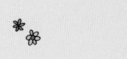

Erase these lines.

1. Use a pencil to draw the outline of a throne. Give it a curved top. Then, draw three steps below it and add lines inside the steps.

2. Draw the Queen's head and hair. Add her dress and wings, overlapping the throne. Then, erase the lines inside the wings and dress.

3. Draw the face and add a crown on top of her head. Draw her sleeves and hands on top of her wings, and add a wand in one hand.

4. Fill in your drawing with paints or felt-tip pens. Draw hearts on the Queen and her throne. Then, add fairies and flowers around her.

Glittery star chain

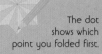
Cut the paper at an angle, like this.

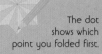
The dot shows which point you folded first.

1. Using a pencil, draw around a mug on a piece of paper. Then, cut out the circle you have drawn.

2. Fold the circle in half. Fold it three more times. Then, cut the folded paper to make a point.

3. Unfold the star. Draw a dot on one point. Fold the star in half from the dot to the opposite point.

4. Crease the fold, then open out the star. Then, fold all the other points in the same way.

5. Pinch two points together and push down the fold in the middle. Repeat this all around the star.

6. Unfold the star and gently press its middle, to open it out a little. Then, make more stars.

Let the glue dry.

Use a long piece of thread.

Hang up the chain.

7. Brush a star with white glue. Sprinkle it with glitter. Glue beads and sequins on the other stars.

8. Turn a star over and dab glue onto two opposite points. Then, lay a piece of thread on the glue.

9. Glue more stars onto the thread, then let the glue dry. Cut off the bottom end of the thread.

83

Tissue paper flowers

1. For petals, fold a piece of tissue paper in half, then in half twice more. Draw a heart and cut it out.

2. For a stem, push a pipe cleaner through one of the petals, like this. Slide the petal down a little.

3. Thread on the rest of the petals. Gently spread them out around the stem to make a flower.

The heart should be this way up.

4. Holding the petals from below, wrap sticky tape around them and press the tape onto the stem.

5. For a leaf, fold a piece of tissue paper in half. Draw a heart on it, then cut out the shape.

6. Cut another pipe cleaner in half. Spread glue on one leaf, then lay the pipe cleaner on top.

You could make some flowers with more than one leaf.

7. Press the other leaf on top and let the glue dry. Then, gently brush white glue over the leaf.

8. Sprinkle glitter on the glue and let it dry. Then, twist the leaf stem around the main stem.

85

Decorations picture

Make the lines cross each other.

1. Use silver paint to paint several curved lines for branches along the top of a piece of paper.

2. Add lots of thinner lines on both sides of the branches, for twigs. Then, leave the paint to dry.

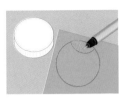

3. Draw around a lid on pink paper. Draw a curved line inside the circle, then fill it in with a gold pen.

4. Draw red spots on the rest of the circle. Draw a silver line around each one, then add petals.

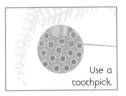
Use a toothpick.

5. Cut out the circle and glue it below a branch. Then, dot white glue onto the red spots, like this.

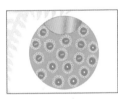

6. While the glue is still wet, carefully press a little bead or sequin onto each dot of glue.

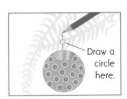
Draw a circle here.

7. Use a red pencil to draw a line for a thread, from the decoration to the top of the paper.

8. Tie a ribbon into a bow and glue it onto the red line. Make lots more decorations and glue them on.

You could make a pointed decoration, like this one.

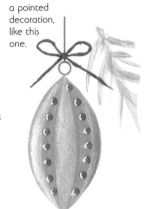

87

Snowflake giftwrap

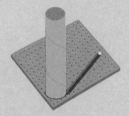

1. Put a cardboard tube on a piece of sponge cloth and draw around it with a pen. If you don't have a tube, use a small jar lid.

2. Using the pen, draw an 'X' shape inside the circle, touching the edges. Then, add a '+' over the top, to make a snowflake shape.

3. To make a snowflake, cut out the circle. Then, cut little triangles from between the lines, but don't cut all the way to the middle.

Spread the glue on the side that you drew on.

4. Lay the cardboard tube on a piece of cardboard and draw around it. Cut out the circle, then glue on the snowflake with white glue.

If you don't have a cork, use a plastic bottle top instead.

Let the paper dry before using it to wrap gifts.

5. Spread white glue on one end of a cork. Press the cork onto the middle of the cardboard circle, then leave the glue to dry completely.

6. Holding the cork, dip the snowflake into thick white paint. Press it onto a big piece of thin paper, then print lots more snowflakes.

Spangly star wand

1. Draw a star on a piece of cardboard and cut it out. Lay it on the cardboard and draw around it.

2. Using a pencil, draw a mark at the top of each star, like this. Then, cut out the second star.

Keep the marks at the top.

3. Cut slots halfway into the stars, like this. Make them the same thickness as the cardboard.

4. Cut a rectangle from kitchen foil, several times wider and a little longer than a straw.

Lay the foil on an old newspaper.

5. Spread glue on the non-shiny side of the foil. Then, lay the straw on top, near one edge.

Flatten the end of the straw.

6. Roll the straw, to cover it with the foil. Then, tape it onto the star with a slot at the top.

Hold the straw in place.

7. Hold the stars with their slots facing each other. Then, slot them together, like this.

Use white glue.

8. Rip lots of pieces of tissue paper and glue them all over the stars. Then, add two more layers.

9. Brush the stars with glue and sprinkle them with glitter. Then, glue on beads and sequins, too.

Flower wall-hanging

1. Using a pencil, draw around a plate on a piece of thick white cardboard. Cut out the circle.

2. Draw a line across the circle. Then, draw the outline of a rainbow and the sun at the top.

3. Add stripes on the rainbow and lines for the sun's rays. Fill in the rainbow with bright paints.

4. Paint the sun, the rays and the ground with bright paints. Then, let the paint dry.

5. Draw flowers on white paper and cut them out. Paint yellow dots on them, then glue them on.

6. Using the point of a ballpoint pen, make a small hole near the top of the painted circle.

Don't glue flowers at the top.

7. Cut nine long pieces of thin ribbon and glue flowers onto them. Leave the glue to dry.

8. Tape the pieces of ribbon around the bottom of the circle, leaving gaps between them.

9. To hang it up, thread a piece of ribbon through the hole at the top and tie a knot in it.

Shiny picture frame

1. Cut a large piece of kitchen foil. Spread glue over the non-shiny side, then fold the foil in half.

2. Rub the foil to make the layers stick together. When it is smooth, lay it on an old magazine.

3. Pressing hard with a ballpoint pen, draw a rectangle on the foil. Add a smaller rectangle inside it.

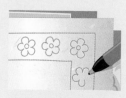

4. Draw lots of flowers between the lines. Cut around the big rectangle, a little way from the line.

5. Push the ballpoint pen through the foil, to make a hole. Cut around the inside line, like this.

6. Lay the frame on thin cardboard. Draw a bigger rectangle around it, like this, then cut it out.

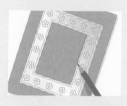

7. Lay the frame on the cardboard again and draw around the hole. Push a pen through the middle.

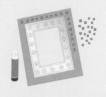

8. Cut out the middle, then glue the foil frame onto the cardboard one. Glue on paper squares.

9. Tape a picture to the back of the frame, facing down. Then, tape a loop of string at the top.

Glitter bugs

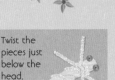

1. Cut a foil square as large as your hand and roll it. Flatten one end and glue on sequins for eyes.

2. Wind a pipe cleaner along the body, like this. You will need the extra part at the end.

Don't cut off this end.

3. Cut another pipe cleaner in half. Twist each half around the body. Then, bend the ends out, like this.

Twist the pieces just below the head.

4. For wings, lay a leaf on newspaper, with its veins facing up. Brush it with silver or gold paint.

5. Using the leaf, print four wings onto two shades of tissue paper. When they are dry, cut them out.

6. Lay the wings, painted side down. Carefully place the bug on top, upside down, like this.

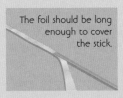

7. Tape the pipe cleaners onto the wings. Bend the pipe cleaners to pull the wings apart.

8. Tape the end of a strip of foil to one end of a kebab stick. Wrap the foil around it, then tape it.

The foil should be long enough to cover the stick.

9. Lay the blunt end of the stick next to the body. Wind the extra pipe cleaner around the stick.

Tissue paper prints

1. Mix some green paint with water on a plate, to make it runny. Brush the paint evenly over a piece of paper.

2. Using a pencil, draw a heart on a piece of red tissue paper. Cut it out, then press it onto the wet paint.

3. Leave the tissue paper heart on the paint for a minute. Then, carefully peel it off, to leave a printed heart.

4. Print more hearts in the same way. Then, use thick paint to add a heart shape on some of them, like this.

Other ideas

Print a strawberry shape instead of a heart. Let it dry, then paint white spots on it and add a green leaf.

You could print a simple flower, then paint a white spot in the middle. Add little white dots around it, too.

Zigzag castle card

Middle fold

Keep both pieces.

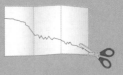

1. Fold a long rectangle of thick paper in half. Then, fold the top layer in half again, like this.

2. Turn the paper over, fold it in the same way, then unfold it. Cut off the left-hand part.

3. Using a pencil, draw a wavy line diagonally across the card, like this. Cut along the line.

Use a thin paintbrush.

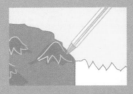

4. Paint the right-hand part green. When it is dry, paint tiny flowers on it.

5. Use purple paint to add mountains. When they are dry, outline the peaks with a silver pen.

6. Turn the card over and paint the middle part green. Cut out green paper trees and glue them on.

7. Paint a castle on the paper from step 2. Let it dry, then outline it with black pen, and cut it out.

8. Fold the paper into a zigzag again. Then, glue the castle near the top of the mountains.

You could make a castle like this one instead.

Sparkly chains

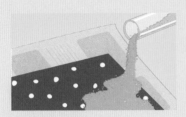

1. Dab lots of small blobs of white glue all over a large piece of bright paper. Then, sprinkle glitter all over the wet glue, like this.

2. When the glue is dry, tip the extra glitter onto an old newspaper. Then, use the glitter to decorate another piece of bright paper.

Make sure that the glitter is on the outside.

3. Leave the glue to dry. Then, use scissors to cut both pieces of paper into lots of strips. Make all the strips the same width.

4. Bend one of the strips into a loop. Secure the join with a piece of sticky tape. Then, thread another strip through the loop and tape it.

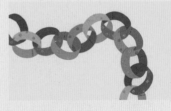

5. Thread another strip through the loop and tape it in place. Continue until you have used all the strips, then hang up the chain.

To make a chain like this one, sprinkle several pieces of paper with different shades of glitter. You could use glitter glue, too.

Sequin card

1. Cut two squares of clear book covering film. Make them the same size. Then, peel the backing paper off one of them.

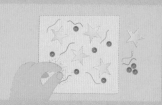

2. Lay the film on a table, sticky-side up. Press lots of sequins and little pieces of thread onto the film. Then, sprinkle on some glitter.

3. Peel the backing paper off the other piece of film. Carefully lay it on top of the decorated piece of film, with its sticky side facing down.

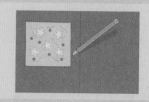

4. For the card, fold a piece of thick paper in half, then open it out. Lay the film on the left-hand side of the card and draw around it.

5. Make a hole in the middle of the square with a pencil or pen, then push a scissor blade through it. Cut a 'window' smaller than the square.

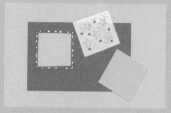

6. Spread glue around the 'window' and press on the decorated film. Then, cut a square of paper and glue it on top, to cover the film.

Fairy rosettes

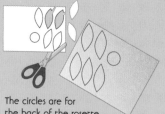

The circles are for the back of the rosette.

1. Draw five petal shapes and a circle on a piece of thin cardboard. Cut them out. Then, cut five slightly larger petals and a circle from foil.

2. Glue each cardboard petal onto a foil petal, then fold the edges over, like this. Cover the circle, too. Then, bend each petal to make a curve.

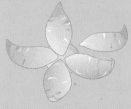

3. Roll one end of a curved petal around a pencil, like this, to make it curl up. Then, do the same to the rest of the petals.

4. Dab a blob of white glue onto the middle of the silver circle. Then, with the foil side facing up, press the petals into the glue, to make a flower.

5. For tendrils, cut three strips of foil and roll them to make thin sticks. Wind the foil sticks around a pencil to make coils, like this.

6. Tape the coiled tendrils to the back of the rosette. Then, glue a small circle of purple paper onto the middle of the rosette.

Index

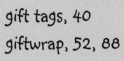

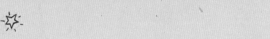

Edited by Minna Lacey. Designed by Amanda Gulliver. Illustrated by Katrina Fearn, Non Figg,
Erica Harrison, Vici Leyhane, Katie Lovell, Jan McCafferty, Antonia Miller, Lucy Parris and Josephine Thompson.
Photographs by Howard Allman. Additional designs by Michelle Lawrence. Digital manipulation by Pete Taylor.
This edition first published in 2014 by Usborne Publishing Ltd, 83-85 Saffron Hill, London, EC1N 8RT, England.
www.usborne.com Copyright © 2014, 2008, 1995 Usborne Publishing Ltd.